East Dunbartonshire Libraries

3 8060 05697 5956

KU-236-447

East Dunbartonshire Council

www.eastdunbarton.gov.uk

weblinks

You don't need a computer to use this book. But, for readers who do have access to the Internet, the book provides links to recommended websites which offer additional information and resources on the subject.

You will find weblinks boxes like this on some pages of the book.

weblinks

For more advice on careers in fashion, go to
www.waylinks.co.uk/
series/soyouwant/fashion

waylinks.co.uk

To help you find the recommended websites easily and quickly, weblinks are provided on our own website, **waylinks.co.uk**. These take you straight to the relevant websites and save you typing in the Internet address yourself.

Internet safety

➚ Never give out personal details, which include: your name, address, school, telephone number, email address, password and mobile number.

➚ Do not respond to messages which make you feel uncomfortable – tell an adult.

➚ Do not arrange to meet in person someone you have met on the Internet.

➚ Never send your picture or anything else to an online friend without a parent's or teacher's permission.

➚ If you see anything that worries you, tell an adult.

A note to adults

Internet use by children should be supervised. We recommend that you install filtering software which blocks unsuitable material.

Website content

The weblinks for this book are checked and updated regularly. However, because of the nature of the Internet, the content of a website may change at any time, or a website may close down without notice. While the Publishers regret any inconvenience this may cause readers, they cannot be responsible for the content of any website other than their own.

HODDER
Wayland

So You Want to Work in

Fashion?

Margaret McAlpine

HODDER
Wayland

an imprint of Hodder Children's Books

EAST ~

Cla~ J331.702

Ba: 38060056975956

Loc~ KIR

Suppli~ HJ

DYNIX Bi. 465644

10/00

£13.99

First published in 2005 by Hodder Wayland,
an imprint of Hodder Children's Books

© Hodder Wayland 2005

Editor: Patience Coster
Inside design: Peta Morey
Cover design: Hodder Wayland

All rights reserved. No part of this publication may be reproduced, stored in a
retrieval system, or transmitted, in any form or by any means without the prior
written permission of the publisher, nor be otherwise circulated in any form of
binding or cover other than that in which it is published and without a similar
condition being imposed on the subsequent purchaser.

British Library Cataloguing Publication Data

McAlpine, Margaret
So you want to work in fashion?
1. Fashion - Vocational guidance - Juvenile literature
2. Models (Persons) - Vocational guidance - Juvenile literature
I. Title
746.9'2'023

ISBN 0 7502 4579 4

Printed in China

Hodder Children's Books
A division of Hodder Headline Limited
338 Euston Road, London NW1 3BH

Picture Acknowledgements. The publishers would like to thank the following for
allowing their pictures to be reproduced in this publication:
Ariel Skelley/Corbis 19 (bottom), 36, 59 (left); Arnaldo Magnani/Getty Images 11;
B.D.V./Corbis 39; Cardinale Stephane/Corbis Sygma 32; Chuck Savage/Corbis 12;
Condé Nast Archive/Corbis 45; Dave G. Houser/Corbis 13; David Raymer/Corbis 48;
Eric Robert/Corbis Sygma 46; Evan Agostini/Getty Images 33; Firefly Productions/
Corbis 56; Frank Pedrick/The Image Works 27; Gail Mooney/Corbis 14, 37, 54;
Henri Tullio/Corbis 30; James Leynse/Corbis 57; Jeremy Bembaron/Corbis Sygma 51
(left); Jose Luis Pelez, Inc./Corbis 16; Jutta Klee/Corbis 29; Kevin Fleming/Corbis 10;
Klaus Lahnstein/Stone/Getty Images 55; LWA-Stephen Welstead/Corbis 6;
Mark Peterson/Corbis 59 (centre); Michael Keller/Corbis 31; Michael S.
Yamashita/Corbis 9; Mitchell Gerber/Corbis 20, 22, 43 (bottom); Owen Franken/Corbis
5; Pace Gregory/Corbis Sygma 25; Patrick Riviere/Getty Images 28;
Patrick Ward/Corbis 43 (top); Paul A. Souders/Corbis 7; Peter Barrett/Corbis 40;
Peter Kramer/Getty Images 49; Petre Buzoianu/Corbis 21; Rick Gomez/Corbis 19 (top);
Roger Ball/Corbis 17; Sean Gallup/Getty Images 4; Siemoneit Ronald/Corbis Sygma 51
(centre); Stephanie Diani/Corbis 23; Steve Chenn/Corbis 15; Steve Finn/Getty Images
35; Steven E. Frischling/Corbis 52; The Image Works/Topham 44; TopFoto/UPPA 26;
Toru Yamanaka/AFP/Getty Images 24; Valerio De Berardinis/Corbis 53; Vo Trung
Dung/Corbis Sygma 8; Yves Forestier/Corbis Sygma 38, 41; Zack Seckler/Corbis 47;
Zoran Milich/Getty Images 34.

Note: Photographs illustrating the 'day in the life of' pages are posed by models

Contents

Words in **bold** can be found in the glossary.

Display Designer/ Visual Merchandiser

What is a display designer/visual merchandiser?

The job of a display designer or visual merchandiser is to attract customers into a shop. He or she achieves this by creating exciting, inviting window displays. Once the customers are inside the shop, they need to be persuaded to stay and make purchases. Designers therefore arrange smaller displays in different departments to tempt customers to buy the goods. Display designers also work in places such as hotels, cinemas and on exhibitions, where interesting displays are good for business.

Depending on the department or store they work in, display designers pull together different objects to create a complete look. For example, designers in a home furnishing store may feature a dining room display, with table, chairs, napkins, china and cutlery. In a clothes shop, a dress on a hanger may not attract much attention. But when it is shown on a dummy model with **accessories** such as shoes and jewellery, it can look very eye-catching and gives customers an idea of how the dress might look on them.

Attractive window displays bring customers into a store. Many stores have a strong, individual look that customers recognize immediately without having to read the name above the window.

Plate-glass windows

In 1834, the British manufacturer Robert Lucas Chance used a process developed in Germany to produce large panes of glass. This process was used widely to make plate-glass windows, which meant that goods in shops could be arranged in large displays to attract the attention of passers-by.

Displays need to be changed regularly to keep customers' interest and many are designed to reflect different seasons and festivals. For example, Christmas displays may feature special festive foods, gifts, and clothes.

In large shopping malls, like this one in the USA, stores need to advertise their goods against stiff competition. Customers are likely to be attracted to the more striking window displays, so good design is all-important.

The various branches of **chain stores** need to look very similar to encourage recognition and **brand loyalty** among customers. Displays for these stores are designed at head office and the instructions and materials are sent out to different branches. The display designers then set them up, following head office's instructions.

Main tasks of a display designer/visual merchandiser

Display designers are responsible for the initial impression made by a shop or department store. Creating an atmosphere that customers will appreciate and enjoy takes a lot of work. For example, the atmosphere might consist of a relaxed country style, using pale wood and soft colours. Or it could be a bold, futuristic look, using black-and-white materials and **chrome** fittings. Whatever the style of a store, the displays need to reflect it.

Choosing the fabric for a display is not easy. The designer must consider the colour and texture of the fabric and needs to have a clear idea of the mood she wants to convey.

At the planning stage, designers work closely with store managers and **buyers** to decide on:
- displays that will most appeal to customers;
- the budget for each display;
- dates during which a display will run.

The designer then:
- sketches some initial designs by hand, or creates them using a **computer-aided design** programme;
- shows the initial designs to the store managers and other members of staff for approval;

Good points and bad points

'My job is very creative which is great. But it can be difficult pleasing everybody. Sales managers often have products they want to promote and bringing all these together in an eye-catching display isn't easy.'

- sources the materials needed to make the approved display.

Designers often put together much of the display themselves. Some displays may be quite simple, for example, using elements such as a draped backdrop and blown-up photographs. Others create an elaborate scene or series of scenes linked together and telling a story. Many stores now use what is known as retail theatre, which means a display theme is carried through the entire store. Once a display is in place, design staff are responsible for keeping it clean and fresh, for carrying out any repairs and, finally, for taking it down.

This window display designer is dressing a **mannequin** in a boutique in Vancouver, Canada.

Skills needed to be a display designer

Artistic skills
Display designers need to be creative and artistic, with a good eye for colour and composition.

Imagination
Designers need to be able to come up with plenty of new ideas for eye-catching displays.

Computer skills
Today, the use of computer-aided design programmes is widespread, so display designers need to be confident computer users.

Designers often sketch out their ideas for the more complicated displays.

Practical skills
Although stores employ carpenters and electricians to help with the **installation** of large displays, all but the most senior designers working for large stores or retail chains are expected to work on the displays themselves.

The work includes:
- using tools such as **chisels** and hammers to construct the displays;
- understanding how lighting systems work;
- dressing models, setting up furniture and arranging flowers and other props.

Stamina
Designers are on their feet for much of the day, bending, lifting and stretching. They need lots of energy because the work can be physically tiring.

Teamwork

Designers need to be able to work alongside others. For example, they need to discuss with buyers and managers what they want to achieve from a display before they start to design it. They also work closely with other people throughout the project.

Communication skills

Designers need to talk over their designs and listen closely to other people's ideas.

Tact

Designers may have to explain why other people's ideas would not work in a display. They need to be able to do this tactfully and without causing offence.

fact file

Display designers need to have taken a degree or a diploma in a subject such as retail design, display design or visual merchandising. In order to gain a place on such a course, students need to have put together a good **portfolio** of their own art and design work.

A menswear display in Florence, Italy: displays such as this, positioned throughout the store, help to increase sales.

A day in the life of a display designer

Robert Morden

Robert is a junior display designer with a large department store. He is one of three young designers working under a senior display designer. He took up his present job after leaving college.

8.30 am   I'm at work early today, so I walk around the outside of the store checking the window displays. A couple of dummies need some adjustment.

9.30 am   The emergency repairs are done and I'm in a meeting where the design and financial teams are talking over the display budget.

11.00 am   I receive a phone call from the eveningwear department. A customer wants to purchase the dress on display. Dresses aren't usually sold from the display stand, but this customer has been let down by her dressmaker and doesn't have time to order a new dress. Our store doesn't have another of these dresses in stock, so the manager phones through to our store in a neighbouring town to see if it has one. I talk to my boss about finding a replacement if the dress on display is to be sold.

Window displays tend to be guided by the seasons – in this case Christmas!

This New York City department store used real people as models in its Christmas 2000 window display. Each of the store windows focussed on a decade from the twentieth century.

12.00 pm Customer service wins the day, and the dress is sold. I start to dismantle the display, removing all the pins and packing without causing any damage.

1.30 pm I have a quick lunch and think over my new display. It doesn't involve a complete window, but the accessories will need to be changed.

2.15 pm The manager shows me three dresses. I make a final decision and choose new accessories and props from different departments in the store.

4.45 pm My boss sees the display and says I've done a good job, so the day has a happy ending.

5.15 pm I clear away, putting my pins, foam pads and other display materials back into my work box.

Fashion Designer

What is a fashion designer?

Fashion designers develop new ideas for clothes, which are then produced and manufactured for sale. The world of fashion is dependent upon trends. One year a particular colour is seen everywhere, the next year perhaps tartan or **paisley** or another distinctive print is in fashion, the next year silks or embroidered fabrics may be fashionable. Designers need to make sure their collections of designs reflect popular trends, so they need to research and think carefully before starting on the design work.

Fashion designers have to select fabrics for their designs. They need to be aware of which textures and colours are fashionable from one season to the next.

It takes about two years for a designer to develop an idea and for the finished garment to appear in the shops. This means, for example, that in winter 2005 designers are beginning to develop ideas for clothes that will appear on sale in winter 2007.

Fashion designers visit trade fairs, exhibitions and fashions shows to find out which styles, fabrics and colours are likely to be popular. This way they can combine their design ideas with current trends.

The New Look

In February 1947, the French fashion designer Christian Dior created a sensation with his 'New Look' collection. After the difficult years of the Second World War people were ready for some relaxation and fun. Dior's longer, fuller skirts, feminine jackets and smart, high-heeled shoes were an immediate success and were copied by women across the world.

Fashion design falls into different groups:

- **haute couture** – where garments are individually designed and cost thousands of pounds;
- **designer label** or **ready-to-wear** collections – where designs are produced in small numbers and sold at high prices in exclusive shops or stores;
- mass production or **high street fashion** – where designs are manufactured in large numbers and sold at reasonable prices in shops nationwide (this is the area in which most people are employed);
- craft and small business – where designers work alone or in small teams, creating their own designs and finding outlets to sell them.

This Chanel store is in Miami, Florida. It is the ambition of many designers to work for one of the world's great fashion houses.

Main tasks of a fashion designer

Designers often specialize in a particular branch of fashion. They may be involved in designing outerwear – coats and jackets – or light clothing, such as dresses, suits and **separates**. They may design evening or wedding dresses or they may specialize in menswear and knitwear.

Whichever area they work in, designers sketch their early designs either on paper or on a computer screen. As they work, they need to consider different fabrics and colours and whether the various elements of the design will work together. For example, how will a wool fabric look trimmed with leather? Will green look good alongside the season's fashionable yellow colour?

Some designers specialize in creating exciting, unusual and beautiful shoes.

Good points and bad points

'The fashion industry is so exciting and I get a real buzz out of being part of it. I visit exhibitions and meet loads of great people.'

'Many people want to work in fashion because it looks so glamorous, and that makes it very competitive. I'm only as good as my last piece of work and that does worry me.'

Designers working for large fashion houses will have a team of garment workers to carry out the practical work. Designers like the ones in the picture who run their own small businesses will do the cutting out and sewing themselves.

The next step is to make up the most promising of these designs and try them on models. In large organizations, garment workers do the making-up work, but in small companies designers do it themselves. At this stage, lots of changes are made and styles are adapted, because clothes look very different on a real, **three-dimensional** person than they do sketched on a page. In the high street fashion industry, sample garments are made up and shown to possible buyers. The most popular styles then go forward for production. The designer is still on hand to advise on any changes required by the mass production process.

weblinks

For more information about the qualifications needed to work in fashion design, go to www.waylinks.co.uk/series/soyouwant/fashion

Skills needed to be a fashion designer

Artistic skills

Designers need to be both creative and original to keep one step ahead of other designers and produce fresh lively designs that reflect the mood of the moment. Sometimes a film or an event captures the public imagination and fashion designs reflect this. At other times, clothes reflect a geographical area such as Africa or the Far East. Designers need to consider current interests and turn them into fashion designs.

Technical skills

Designers need the technical skill to make their ideas reality. These skills involve:

● making patterns;
● a good knowledge of different fabrics and how they can be used;
● the ability to sew (in order to understand the methods and techniques that can be used).

Designers may find it useful to discuss their ideas with their colleagues. Many designs, however, are closely guarded secrets.

Computer skills

It is essential for designers to be confident using computer-aided design programmes, so that they can make changes to their designs quickly. For example, on a computer a designer can see almost immediately how different colours look when used together, or how the inclusion of long sleeves could change the appearance of a dress.

Interest in fashion

Designers must keep in touch with the latest trends. They have to analyze the work of top designers, including those in different parts of the world.

Self-confidence

The fashion industry is tough and competitive. Designers need to believe in their own ability so that they can cope with criticism and disappointment.

Discipline

Designers need to be able to meet deadlines and keep to budgets.

Communication skills

Designers have to be able to explain and describe their work to other people.

fact file

The way into fashion design is to take a degree or a diploma in a subject such as art and design or fashion. There is a great deal of competition for jobs, and young designers can expect to spend several years working in junior positions on other people's designs before gaining jobs as designers themselves.

Students of fashion design must spend time learning the basics of measuring, cutting and sewing patterns and understanding the uses of different fabrics.

A day in the life of a fashion designer

Susie Harris

Susie runs her own business, designing and making wedding and evening dresses. After leaving college, she worked for a company specializing in eveningwear. After five years, she felt she had learned enough about the design and business side of the work to set up her own company.

7.30 am   I'm making alterations to a dress, because the bride has suddenly lost a lot of weight.

9.00 am   I visit one of my out-workers to talk about new assignments. I do a lot of sewing, especially the fine detail such as embroidery. However, I also need top-class people to sew for me. So far, I have a team of three.

11.00 am   I have an appointment with a new client and her mother. They have cut out pictures from magazines, drawn sketches and collected fabric samples, so they are quite clear about what they want. The fabric they have in mind is rather too heavy for the style, which has a full skirt and fitted waist. I explain that there could be a problem and suggest I find new fabric samples.

1.00 pm   No time for lunch – I eat a packet of crisps in the car.

2.00 pm   I meet with a journalist who wants to interview me for a magazine article. One of my dresses was worn to a big wedding, and this is why the magazine has picked up on my name. A photographer from the magazine is coming out to see me next week, which is great!

4.30 pm   I am back at the cutting table. I need to finish cutting out the pattern for this evening dress today so that I can deliver the pieces to my sewing team.

6.00 pm   I receive a phone call from someone who wants me to design a ball gown. It's been a good day.

Clients may have firm ideas of what fabrics and styles they want before they meet the designer.

Designers are often self-employed and handle all the various areas of their businesses, including taking and making-up orders.

Fashion Make-up Artist and Hairstylist

What is a fashion make-up artist and hairstylist?

Fashion make-up artists and hairstylists apply models' make-up and style their hair for fashion photo shoots and shows. A quick look at any fashion photograph shows the importance of make-up and hairstyling in the fashion world. In everyday life, make-up and hairstyles are usually **subtle** and practical, but fashion styles are much more elaborate and designed to enhance the clothes being worn. In some cases, the hairstyles and make-up worn in fashion shows and photographs are quite theatrical, with stunning, unreal designs creating an air of complete fantasy.

A fashion model waits backstage at a show for her make-up artist to arrive.

In the fashion world, hair and make-up styling are usually undertaken by the same person, who is skilled at doing both jobs. One of the biggest differences between working in a salon and in the fashion industry is the speed at which stylists work. In a salon, stylists can take time making sure the customer is satisfied with the result of their work. In the fashion industry they need to work

The history of make-up

For thousands of years women and, sometimes, men have used make-up to improve their appearance. In Ancient Greece, Rome and Egypt, women used white lead and chalk on their faces. Egyptians used black **kohl** eyeliner to make their eyes look bigger, while Persians stained their hair and faces with **henna** dye. Wigs and hair extensions were used by women throughout the ancient world.

A make-up artist works on a model for the Christian Dior autumn 2004 collection. Fashion make-up can be very elaborate and takes a great deal of advance planning.

quickly to alter hairstyles and make-up in few moments to match different outfits. In a salon, stylists ask the customers how they would like to look. Fashion stylists, however, take their instructions from the designers, photographers, magazine editors or whoever is paying them to do the work.

Fashion stylists usually work on a **freelance** basis and are taken on for a particular job. They need to be prepared to travel to wherever there is work.

Make-up artists work both in **catwalk** or **runway** modelling and photographic modelling.

● When they are **commissioned** to do a job, make-up artists meet with the rest of the team of designers, photographers and lighting engineers to discuss what is required. Their brief (instructions) could include creating a look to match an overall theme – for example, giving models an Oriental appearance or a futuristic look. They may be asked to undertake special effects – for

Fashion model Claudia Schiffer talks over what is required for a fashion show with her make-up artist.

Good points and bad points

'What I do like is the creative side of my work. A face is like a blank piece of paper, waiting for me to start work on it. '

'I do get tired of people telling me how glamorous my job must be and how they'd love to meet so many famous people. One face is very similar to another, and there isn't a lot of chance to chat when putting on someone's make-up.'

example, producing a windblown or sun-tanned look for a photographic session. Or they may be asked to create natural looking make-up and hairstyles for advertisement shots.

- Where a particular effect is required, the stylist works out some ideas, discusses these with the rest of the team and practises the hair and make-up designs on models to achieve the best effect.

On the day of the shoot or the show, the stylist arrives early to set out make-up and equipment, check the notes of work to be done and discuss last-minute changes with the rest of the team. Once these tasks are complete, the job can begin.

A fashion designer (centre) talks with a model (left) while a make-up artist covers the model's legs with 'base', a kind of tan powder.

- Where complex special effects are required, stylists work from sketches and photographs to make sure they create the right look. Throughout photographic shoots and catwalk shows, they are on hand to repair make-up and hair and to adapt styles where necessary.

Skills needed to be a fashion make-up artist and hairstylist

Artistic skills

Stylists need to be able to visualize how their creations will look before they begin work on them. They use make-up in the way that artists use paint or crayons, to create something original and eye-catching.

Practical skills

Stylists need to have good ideas, but they also need to be able to turn these into reality. This means being able to use different types of make-up in a competent, professional way and styling hair into whatever look is required. Time is limited on fashion shoots and at fashion shows and make-up artists need to work very quickly, without making mistakes.

Stamina

Fashion make-up artists spend most of the day on their feet, often working in uncomfortable conditions. They also have to carry round heavy cases full of make-up and equipment.

At the 'Bridal Model' contest in Tokyo, Japan, in 2004, make-up artists are at the ready to carry out repair work. In this annual contest, some 62 artists compete to coordinate make-up, hairstyling, ornaments and costumes.

Tact and patience

To do their job well, stylists need to be able to get on with everyone. Models may be nervous before a show and make-up artists need to help them relax, so they can apply their make-up and do their hair swiftly and to a high standard.

Supermodel of the 1970s, Lauren Hutton, used the tricks she learned from forty years of working with the world's best make-up artists to create her own line of cosmetics and skin-care products.

fact file

There are diploma and degree courses in fashion hair and make-up. Many stylists learn about hairstyling and make-up by taking an apprenticeship and working on the job before specializing in fashion and make-up.

Reliability

Many people would like to break into the fashion make-up world, so there is a great deal of competition. Artists need to build up a reputation for good work, for punctuality and for never letting clients down.

Scientific knowledge

For safety reasons, make-up artists need to know exactly how the products they use can react on skin and hair.

weblinks

For more information on a career in fashion make-up and hairstyling, go to www.waylinks.co.uk/series/ soyouwant/fashion

A day in the life of a make-up artist

Vittorio Dalzetti

Vittorio has been working as a make-up artist for almost five years. He has always worked freelance, which means he is self-employed and has to find his own jobs. It was tough at first, but as he becomes better known, so his work increases.

8.30 am   I'm enjoying my coffee and cleaning out my make-up box, throwing away any pieces of cotton wool or tissue that have found their way in there. I make a list of any products that will soon need replacing. I also check that everything is in the right place. Hunting for an eye-shadow during a make-up session takes precious time and looks disorganized.

10.15 am   Looking through some notes from a meeting yesterday, I think over ways of creating a 1940s look for a show. I dig out some of my fashion books and start jotting down ideas.

12.00 pm   It's taken me a while, but I've got some good ideas which I need to talk over at the next meeting with the show team.

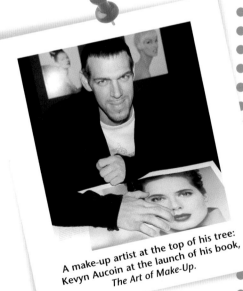

A make-up artist at the top of his tree: Kevyn Aucoin at the launch of his book, The Art of Make-Up.

Creating an elaborate hairstyle like this takes practice, time and skill.

1.00 pm   I have lunch with Sue, an editorial assistant on a big fashion magazine. She gives me some information about possible work.

3.00 pm   I phone a couple of the names Sue has given me and find that both might lead to something positive. I send off my details straightaway.

4.15 pm   I fill in an order for the new make-up I need.

5.00 pm   Tomorrow I'm out all day on a photoshoot. I check the location and work out my best route and how long the journey is likely to take. I always allow myself an extra half-hour to make sure I won't be late.

Fashion Model

What is a fashion model?

The job of a fashion model is to make clothes look as attractive as possible so that people will want to buy them. Clothing companies employ fashion models to wear garments and accessories such as handbags, shoes, gloves and jewellery and to show them off to their best advantage. Models tend to fall into two different categories – **agency** and **showroom**. They work in a variety of situations, including catwalk shows and photographic shoots for magazines and catalogues.

Fashion modelling is a young person's world. Female models need to be between 16 and 18 years of age and male models between 17 and 25 years. Both males and females need to be tall and slim. There are some opportunities for people who do not fit into these groups. They are known as character models and include older people and larger sizes. Most of their

A model parades a new design on an open-air catwalk. Most models are young, tall and very slim.

Twentieth-century style

Coco Chanel was one of the most famous fashion designers of the twentieth century. Born in Saumur, France, in 1883, she revolutionized fashion by showing women that they could look good in shorter skirts, loose designs and soft fabrics instead of long dresses and tight-fitting corsets. In line with her pioneering new look, Chanel had her hair cut in a short, boyish style and wore knee-length skirts and cardigan jackets. Designers are still influenced by Chanel's styles today.

There is photographic work available for models with particularly good features, for example, hands, arms or feet.

work is photographic work for mail order catalogues and advertisements.

Modelling has a glamorous image, but becoming a full-time professional model is highly competitive and difficult. Most models work part-time and have another job or jobs to bring in regular money. Most are self-employed and find work through being registered with a fashion agency.

Main tasks of a fashion model

Most models are agency models. Agencies take models on to their books if they think they are likely to be selected by their clients for work. The agency shows photographs and descriptions of their models to clients. Agency models must be prepared to take all sorts of different work. This may include:

Professional models need to make sure they look their best all the time, which can be expensive.

- Show modelling: major fashion shows take place in cities such as London, New York, Paris and Milan twice a year. This is when most show work is available. Before a show, models have to rehearse catwalk routines. These can be complicated, with models dancing to music and displaying clothes in a

Good points and bad points

'I enjoy modelling. I'm not rich or famous, but I do some show modelling and meet some interesting people. A couple of photographers also use me regularly for catalogue work.'

'Keeping myself looking good costs a fortune. My hair has to be cut and coloured much more often than if I worked in an office and I spend a great deal of money on skin care products and make-up. This isn't because I'm vain but because I have to look my best if I'm going to get work.'

group. They also need to practise quick changes of clothes, hairstyles and make-up, as these are required during a show. Their job during the show is to follow the routines they have practised, to show the clothes off to the audience.

- Photographic modelling: this takes place either in a studio or on location. Photography sessions can last for hours while photographers adjust lighting, clothes and poses. Types of work include fashion magazine photography (the top level of modelling, only reached by a few), mail order catalogue photography and advertisement and poster photography.

Showroom models are employed by fashion houses and paid a regular salary. Their work includes trying on clothes so that designers can carry out alterations. They also wear clothes to show to buyers, personal customers and fashion journalists, and talk about the details of the clothes and answer questions. Showroom models also work at large fashion shows (although many fashion houses use freelance models for this type of work). When they are not modelling, showroom models do jobs such as answering the phone and dealing with customers' requests.

Mail order catalogues provide a lot of work for photographic models.

Skills needed to be a fashion model

Attractive physical appearance
Models need to be of a certain height, weight and age, with the type of looks that are currently popular. One year, long, curly hair can be in demand and the next year straight hair may be popular. Weight gain can mean loss of work, so models need to make sure they don't put on even a few pounds.

Determination
Good looks and the right build are not enough for a successful modelling career. Only those who are prepared to put their career before everything else are likely to succeed. The careers of even the most successful models rarely last longer than a few years.

Commitment
Models must be prepared to work long hours and travel long distances often at short notice. They spend a lot of time following other people's instructions, standing or walking in a certain way or taking up a particular position.

Energy
The work is tough and physically exhausting, yet models always have to smile, be friendly and look as if they are having a great time.

Originally seen as a woman's job, modelling has now become a male occupation too. The same rules and pressures apply, however – models must be tall, slim and even-featured.

A sense of humour is important in a tough world. Here, models relax at a knitting party organized by an agency in New York City.

fact file

A successful career in modelling depends on hard work, natural talent and a great deal of luck. There are no academic requirements necessary. Modelling courses exist, and these teach students the basics; but they are expensive and do nothing to guarantee work.

Financial skills

Most models are self - employed and need to be able to deal sensibly with their own finances.

Confidence

Models need to believe in their own talent and ability in order to cope positively with disappointments.

Good humour and the ability to get on with others

Even among top models, tantrums and bad behaviour are not popular. Word soon spreads if a model is difficult and a bad reputation leads to a shortage of work.

weblinks

For more information on a career in fashion modelling, go to
www.waylinks.co.uk/series/soyouwant/fashion

A day in the life of a fashion model

Lauren Moss

Lauren is eighteen years old and has been working as a fashion model for more than a year. She sent in some photographs of herself to an agency, which took her on to their books and now finds her work. She also has a part-time evening job in a restaurant, which she hopes to give up in a few months when her modelling work has increased.

6.30 am The alarm goes off and I get up and jump into the shower. I live at home and my parents don't charge me any rent. They really support me – I don't think I could manage without them.

7.30 am I've finished doing my hair and make-up and I've packed my overnight bag. I have a cup of tea and a bowl of cereal. Today I'm off to a trade exhibition. The event lasts for three days, with four fashion shows every day. It's an outdoor life exhibition so we'll be wearing jodhpurs, jackets and warm jumpers.

8.00 am I meet a couple of other models at the train station.

10.30 am We arrive at the exhibition centre and are shown the catwalk and changing rooms. We try on our clothes, which is just as well because couple of my tops have to be changed.

Models have to keep themselves slim and fit if they are to continue to find work.

A successful fashion show needs to be thoroughly rehearsed. Changes have to be quick and any damage to make-up and hair repaired in a few seconds.

11.30 am   Rehearsals begin. I have a dozen or so changes and the moves on the catwalk are quite complicated, more like dancing than walking.

1.00 pm   Sandwiches are brought in and we collapse for ten minutes before carrying on with the rehearsal. There are eight of us and we all seem to work well together.

3.00 pm   Stand holders are setting up their displays. Our changing rooms are very chilly probably because the heating won't be turned on until the show opens tomorrow.

5.30 pm   The place is now freezing but we're still at work, trying on clothes and practising our moves. Gradually the show is coming together.

7.30 pm   The bus has arrived to take us to the hotel, where I'm going to have a very hot bath.

Fashion Photographer

What is a fashion photographer?

Fashion photographers are the people who take pictures of models for magazines and advertisements. Fashion photography is seen as the most glamorous area of photography and the one where there is most money to be made, yet only a small amount of a fashion photographer's time is spent taking pictures.

Fashion photographers work with models, stylists and lighting technicians, and spend a great deal of time preparing for a shot and making sure everything is exactly right before the shooting starts. They also spend a lot of time making contacts and trying to find work.

Fashion photographers need to invest in high quality equipment, which is very expensive.

There are two main types of fashion photography. The first is runway or catwalk photography, which involves taking photos at fashion shows. The second is advertising and editorial photography, where the photographer is commissioned to take pictures to accompany printed matter, such as magazine articles.

Most fashion photographers work freelance, which means they are self-employed. They are not paid a

A famous photographer

David Bailey is known throughout the world for his photographs of beautiful women. Born in 1938 in the East End of London, his interest in photography began when he was stationed in Singapore with the Royal Air Force. In 1957 he bought his first camera and within two years had a job as an assistant fashion photographer. A year later, he was taking photographs for magazines such as *Vogue.*

A photographer measures the light levels around a fashion model during a shoot. The right lighting is vital to the quality of a photographer's work.

regular salary but work for a number of different organizations and receive money for each job they do. Occasionally, fashion photographers are lucky enough to be given a contract from a client to take pictures for a certain length of time, perhaps a year.

As in all areas of photography, fashion photographers are moving from conventional to digital cameras and downloading their pictures straight on to computers.

Main tasks of a fashion photographer

Fashion photographers may be commissioned to do a job – this means they are contacted beforehand and asked to take pictures at an event. A price is agreed and a deadline set for the work before the job is done. Alternatively they may work completely freelance – attending an event and taking pictures, which they try to sell afterwards to newspapers and magazines.

There are two types of fashion photography.

- Runway or catwalk photography involves taking pictures at fashion shows. Photographers cover the haute couture and ready-to-wear fashion shows. This can mean photographing several shows on the same day, working from early morning until late at night. Photographers arrive at the **venue** a couple of hours early to get a good position. Between shows, they move their equipment to the next venue.

A studio photoshoot gets underway: fashion models, assistants and equipment are all expensive to hire, so the photographer must work swiftly if he is to keep to budget.

Good points and bad points

'One week I have so much work I barely get any sleep and the next week the phone never seems to ring. But, if you can cope with the insecurity, it's a great life and every day is different.'

'Fashion photography is not a job for the nervous. Unless you are one of the handful of top names, it is an insecure existence.'

- Advertising and editorial photography involves the photographer being commissioned by clients such as newspaper and magazine editors and publicity managers of retail stores. The photos may be taken on location or in a photographic studio.

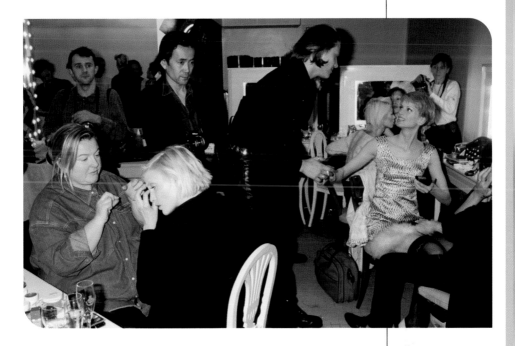

While fashion photographers have their own basic equipment, they also hire equipment for particular jobs, which may need special cameras, lights and **lenses**. Basic photographic equipment can cost around £50,000. Unless they are very well established and have their own studio, fashion photographers hire studios by the day.

On some jobs, fashion photographers need an assistant to run errands, pack and unpack equipment and help set up props and backdrops. Assistants are hired by the day. Most young photographers begin their careers as assistants or 'runners'.

Photographers chat to fashion models backstage at a show. Photographers must pursue their contacts to get work and must be persistent if they are to succeed.

Skills needed to be a fashion photographer

Artistic skill

Fashion photographers need to be creative even when working under pressure. To be successful, they have to know instinctively what will make a good picture.

Technical skill

Photographic equipment develops technically all the time and fashion photographers need to keep up-to-date with the latest developments. They need to know which equipment to buy or hire and they have to use it confidently even in crowded, difficult situations such as fashion shows.

Fashion photography can involve visits to exotic places. While conditions in the studio can be artificially controlled, location photoshoots have additional problems of weather and lighting.

Strong interest in fashion

No one wants to use a photographer who is unaware of fashion trends and doesn't have good ideas about how to show styles at their best.

IT skills

Today all professional photographers use digital photography that allows them to improve pictures and make changes such as cutting out unwanted shadows.

Before proceeding to the final shot, the photographer looks at a **Polaroid** photo of the set-up with a model.

fact file

There is no single way to becoming a fashion photographer. The most usual route is to take a college course in photography, then to try to find work as a photographer's assistant on a fashion shoot. In this way, photographers gain valuable practical experience. To be given assignments, photographers need to build up a portfolio showing the work they have done.

Photographers must keep pace with this new technology.

Business skills

Almost all fashion photographers manage their work alone. They are responsible for booking their own appointments, meeting deadlines, running their own business, controlling finances and working out the fees to charge for a job. This takes time and organizational skills. There is no place in the fashion world for an unreliable photographer.

Interpersonal skills

If they are going to get work, fashion photographers need to be easy and pleasant to get along with.

A day in the life of a fashion photographer

Will Duncan

Will is a freelance fashion photographer. His interest in photography began when he was a teenager. After taking a photography course at college, he was offered a job as an assistant to a fashion photographer. A short time ago, he set up his own freelance business.

8.00 am   I'm in my van with a map and my assistant Roy, who's driving. He's been doing a lot of work for me recently, so he's getting to know how I operate. We're off to a chocolate factory for a magazine fashion shoot. In the fashion world everybody is trying to think of something different, and this is what the editor wants.

9.00 am   Roy unloads the equipment. I go to find the fashion editor and the factory manager.

9.45 am   Together we're coming up with some ideas. None of the machinery will be working during the shoot for safety reasons.

10.30 am   We're using some volunteers from the production staff in the shots. They will be wearing their overalls and providing the necessary background against which the models can pose in their different outfits.

11.00 am   Shooting starts. I'm very glad Roy is here. He's really quick to move lighting and equipment wherever I tell him. He has also come up with some good ideas for interesting shots.

2.30 pm   I use my laptop computer to show the editor the shots I've taken so she can decide what else she needs. The production staff are definitely less keen than they were. They're tired and most of them seem to wish they'd stuck to making chocolate.

4.00 pm   Back to the laptop computer: luckily the editor is satisfied and the day ends on a positive note.

5.00 pm   Roy and I start to load up the van ready for the journey home.

A fashion model is photographed on a beach, while assistants hold up reflectors to shine light on to his face.

Photographers crowd round the catwalk to get a photo of fashion model Kate Moss. After the show, the photographers need to get the pictures to the client as quickly as possible.

weblinks

For more information on a career in fashion photography, go to www.waylinks.co.uk/series/ soyouwant/fashion

Fashion Writer

What is a fashion writer?

Fashion writers are an important link between fashion designers, manufacturers and members of the public. They write articles on fashion for magazines, newspapers and, increasingly, websites. Through their writing, they influence people about what to buy and where to buy it.

Fashion is big business. At one time, clothes were strictly practical. They were usually homemade and only thrown away when they became 'worn out', which meant the fabric was falling into holes. A set of 'Sunday best' clothes was kept for special occasions, but even these were expected to last for a long time.

Today, shops are filled with clothes in the latest colours and styles. Many people buy clothes as soon as a new trend appears in the shops. They no longer feel they should not buy a new sweater because they already have one. They find out the 'must haves' for the next few months through newspapers, magazines and television programmes, which are full of the latest trends and show celebrities wearing them.

Fashion magazines bring the latest trends to their readers.

Keeping in vogue

In the 1950s, high street shops appeared, making fashion items affordable for people on average incomes. Before that date, following fashion had only been possible for the rich. Those wealthy people who could afford haute couture enjoyed keeping up with the latest styles and were interested to find out more about them. In Paris, in 1892, a high fashion magazine called *Vogue* was launched. By the 1920s, *Vogue* was having a strong influence on the fashion scene. Today, the magazine is published in many different languages and read throughout the world.

The cover of *Vogue* from 1929. Styles may have changed over the years, but the job of the fashion magazine has always been to cover the latest trends.

Fashion manufacturers use seasonal changes to launch new lines, and these ensure that clothes are bought throughout the year.

There are magazines devoted entirely to fashion. Teenage magazines and women's magazines have large fashion sections. National newspapers run regular weekly fashion features and fashion programmes are popular television viewing. There is also a growing number of fashion websites.

Main tasks of a fashion writer

Fashion writers need to know exactly what is going on in the fashion world. They do this by:

- making close contacts in the industry – getting to know people who work in different areas of fashion and keeping in regular touch;
- attending fashion shows and trade exhibitions and interviewing people working in the industry;
- carrying out their own research – reading fashion articles in other publications.

Fashion houses and large stores often have public relations (PR) departments, which send out information to the press, deal with questions and arrange for meetings with designers and viewings of the latest designs.

Fashion writers attend shows to view the newest styles and meet professionally with other journalists, designers and buyers.

Good points and bad points

'Being a fashion writer means I get out and about visiting shows and interviewing people in the industry.'

'My work is great fun, but I still have to make sure all my deadlines are met, and this adds to the pressure of the job.'

Using information they have gathered from various fashion houses, fashion writers discuss future articles with their **editor**, making sure they cover what people will want to read. Editors have the final say over what is published and may make last minute changes to a publication. In the case of monthly magazines, articles are written up to four or five months ahead.

Writers work closely with photographers to ensure that the photos accompanying an article are just right. To achieve this, the writers must:
- agree with the photographers on which models and which locations to use;
- contact fashion houses or shops to supply clothes for the models;
- select the photographs to accompany the article.

The length of an article is decided in advance and fashion writers have to keep to a certain number of words. They also have to meet deadlines and finish their work by a set date so that the magazine or newspaper can be printed on time.

Top fashion writers follow events around the world. These journalists are reviewing the Bill Blass spring/ summer 2005 collection in New York.

Skills needed to be a fashion writer

Excellent fashion sense

Every season brings with it new styles and colours. Readers of magazines want to know well in advance what is going to be in the shops in the coming months and they rely on fashion writers to tell them this. Fashion houses, manufacturers and shops all want publicity and work hard to persuade writers to write about them and their creations. Fashion writers need to see beyond the glamour of the fashion world to judge what is likely to appeal to their readers and sell well.

Fashion writers need to liaise with the rest of the creative team about picture selection. As they have witnessed the event at first-hand, they know best which photos reflect the atmosphere.

Writing skills

Fashion writers need to pack a great deal of information into their articles. They also need to write in a way which readers find interesting and easy to follow.

Networking

Fashion writers need to work closely with editors, photographers and page designers. They also need to make excellent contacts within the fashion industry, to make sure they hear all the latest news as quickly as possible.

Organizational skills

Fashion writers need to plan their time with care to cope with busy schedules and meet deadlines for articles.

When a writer becomes an editor: the influential editor of American *Vogue*, Anna Wintour (left), talks to top fashion designer Donna Karan. Whether a writer or an editor, the job is all about contacts.

fact file

It is possible to take a degree in fashion journalism. However, such courses are relatively new and there is no set route into a job in fashion writing. At present, the most usual way in is to move from working in the fashion industry into journalism. Alternatively, some people work as general journalists and then specialize in fashion.

Energy and enthusiasm

Life is busy for fashion journalists both in and out of the office. Fashion writing is definitely not a 9–5 job, but involves staying late at the office to finish work on time. Several evenings a week are likely to be spent being sociable, meeting contacts for meals and drinks and attending fashion events.

IT skills

Today all journalists work on computers. They write articles on screen while working on location and email them to editors as well as using the Internet for information.

weblinks

For more information on a career in fashion journalism, go to www.waylinks.co.uk/series/soyouwant/fashion

A day in the life of a fashion writer

Amy Moran

Amy is a fashion writer with a national newspaper. Her first job after college was as a trainee on a local newspaper. The team working on the paper was small and because of Amy's interest in fashion she was soon given the fashion page to write. Her next job was as assistant fashion editor on a regional paper and from there she went on to her present job.

8.00 am   I'm in the office early to work on an article, which needs to be with my editor by midday.

9.00 am   My phone begins to ring. I tell the receptionist I'm not taking calls. That may sound hard, but unless I'm firm I could be on the phone all day long and do no work at all.

9.30 am   I check my diary to make sure I haven't forgotten to do anything vital.

10.00 am   A photographer arrives with photos taken for my article. Together we choose three or four possibilities.

11.45 am   I check through the article and phone through to the editor. He wants to see me to talk over the way the article is to look and to discuss my ideas for the next month or so.

12.30 pm   I have an early lunch before setting off for an end of term fashion show at a university. These are always lively affairs and a great way of discovering new designers.

4.00 pm   The show was great fun and I single out three students whose designs I would like to feature.

4.15 pm	I interview the students while the photographer takes some shots of their designs.
5.30 pm	I decide to go home and spend the evening working on my article about the students.
9.00 pm	A hot bath, a pizza and a chance to relax in front of the television before bed and another early start tomorrow.

Guests and writers attend a fashion show given by the students of designer Vivienne Westwood. Here, a model shows off one of the student's creations.

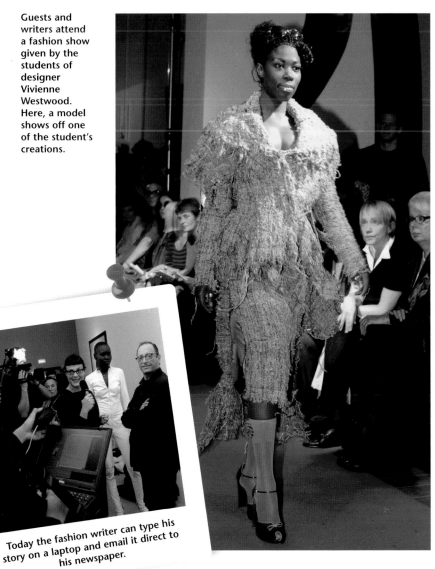

Today the fashion writer can type his story on a laptop and email it direct to his newspaper.

Retail Buyer

What is a retail buyer?

Retail buyers choose the goods that will sell well in a particular shop and this means knowing exactly what customers want. The range of goods available in shops today is enormous and every single item has been selected by a buyer.

In department stores, rapid turnover depends on stocking the right styles. Here, holiday shoppers hurry through the aisles of Macy's in New York City during the sales on the day after Thanksgiving.

Major chain stores have branches in most towns and cities, and they may appear to sell the same clothes in each one. However, the range for each branch has been adapted to meet the tastes of people in that area. The items that quickly sell out in a lively city suburb may stay on the shelf for a long time in a small market town. No matter how skilled the sales staff are, or how eye-catching the displays might be, if a shop does not provide customers with what they want, they will shop somewhere else and the business will fail. Buyers therefore have a lot of responsibility, and must understand their target market very precisely in order to stock the right type of product.

The retail revolution

In 1838, Aristide Boucicaut opened the first department store, called the Bon Marche, in Paris, France. Inside, goods were displayed in different departments, all for sale at a fixed price, with a money-back guarantee and the possibility of exchanges and refunds.

In 1848, Alexander Turney Stewart built his Marble Palace at Broadway and Chambers Street in New York City, selling women's clothes imported from Europe and holding fashion shows for customers.

The buyers need to know exactly what customers like and what they want to buy.

Retail buyers need to keep up-to-date with the latest styles and developments, and with changes of population in their area. For example, the building of a new housing estate or the opening of new factories or offices will bring new people into an area. This may mean a change in the type of goods being sold in local shops.

Main tasks of a retail buyer

Fashion buyers have to keep up with the latest trends. They do this by reading fashion magazines and articles, keeping a sharp eye on goods in other stores, attending fashion shows and trade fairs, and meeting staff from fashion houses and manufacturing companies.

Stores place orders well ahead of the time the goods appear on the sales floor. Firstly buyers need to assess the budget for a season and the type of clothes that are likely to sell well. They need to discuss these issues with the fashion sales manager and other members of the store's management team.

Choosing the right fabric at a reasonable price is part of a buyer's job. So is finding unusual and fashionable prints and colours.

Good points and bad points

'I travel quite a lot with my job, which I enjoy, because it means every day is different. I like identifying new trends and making decisions about what to buy.'

'I do worry about the responsibilities I have, spending a lot of money that isn't mine. I need to be adventurous and find clothes that are new and different, but I also have to put myself in my customers' place and think of what they want. If I make too many bad choices, I could be out of a job.'

Some buyers fly around the world looking for the right products.

Secondly, armed with the information they need, the buyers attend fashion shows and hold meetings with manufacturers to find the styles that are right for their store. They also discuss prices, which usually depend on the size of an order – the larger the order, the lower the price of an individual item.

Buyers present their suggestions to the store's senior sales staff. Once a decision has been made, they place an order for the goods with the manufacturer and sign a contract for delivery. When the order has been placed, the buyer makes sure that the terms of the contract are met. The buyer's responsibilities here include ensuring that the right number of goods have been made in agreed colours and sizes; checking that the goods have been made to a good standard; and the goods being delivered at the right time and to the right place.

When the goods are on the shop floor and being sold, the buyer monitors sales to find out whether the items are popular with customers and selling well.

Skills needed to be a retail buyer

Up-to-date knowledge of fashion
Buyers must decide which popular styles will sell well and make sure that they are in their stores. They need to combine a good sense of fashion with knowledge of the type of clothes their customers will like. There is little point in stocking outrageously fashionable items if the buyer knows that his or her customers will always opt for more conventional styles.

Strong local market awareness
Buyers can only choose the right products if they understand their customers and know their tastes and what they will want to buy. This knowledge comes from looking carefully at past sales figures, talking to sales managers and keeping up-to-date with any changes in the neighbourhood, such as the building of new houses.

Sales meetings give buyers a chance to get up-to-date with sales managers and other members of staff.

Communication skills
Buyers spend a great deal of time dealing with people and negotiating agreements. They need to have a friendly manner and be able to explain clearly exactly what they are looking for.

Commitment
Buyers must be prepared to work long hours, travel a great deal, sometimes abroad, and spend time away from home.

Items that do not sell quickly have to be sold at a reduced price.

Organizational skills

A buyer's days are busy and involve meetings with different people in different places. Buyers need to plan their time carefully and keep to a strict schedule.

Problem-solving skills

The work can be stressful, for example, when deliveries are late or when a particular style does not sell as well as expected. Buyers have to deal with difficulties without being overwhelmed by them.

fact file

There are degrees in subjects such as retail management and marketing, which can lead eventually to a job as a buyer. However, graduates still need sales experience on the shop floor and practical in-house training before they can apply to become a buyer.

A day in the life of a retail buyer

Julia James

Julia is senior fashion buyer with a large department store. She joined the company as a sales assistant and worked her way up to the position of buyer.

9.00 am   There's a lot to do because this afternoon I'm leaving on a trip to visit fashion houses and manufacturers in different parts of Europe.

We sell a wide range of fashions, from teenage styles to exclusive evening and wedding dresses. I'm in overall charge of fashion buying, although I have a team of three buyers working with me. One of them will be coming on the trip.

9.30 am   I attend a meeting with other fashion buyers and managers. There's a lot to discuss including the coming seasonal sale. Each department manager reports on his or her plans. Sales are a good chance of bringing in the customers and getting rid of old stock. But pricing has to be keen, as we can't afford to lose too much money.

11.30 am   Last-minute changes to my schedule mean that an important meeting with a manufacturer has to be changed. He is one of the key people I want to see, so I'm on the phone for the next couple of hours re-scheduling three days of my trip.

1.30 pm   I take a late lunch as I check through my paperwork and memorize as many facts and figures as I can. My budget is tight and I'm going to have to spend my money wisely.

2.30 pm The manager of the wedding dress department rings to find out if we can guarantee a three-month delivery on a certain style. The dresses are made individually for each customer and three months is quite tight. I make some phone calls and check delivery dates.

3.45 pm We're on our way to the airport. I make some notes in the taxi and discuss with my colleague some ideas for the next few days.

5.15 pm The flight will be called in the next five minutes, so it's time to find passports and boarding passes.

Designer Victor Alfaro (left) works to convince fashion buyer June Horne (centre) of the saleable qualities of one of his dresses.

A successful sale is always good news to a retail buyer.

weblinks

For more information on a career in retail buying, go to www.waylinks.co.uk/series/soyouwant/fashion

Glossary

accessories – small, accompanying items of dress, for example, shoes, gloves, handbags, jewellery.

agency modelling – a type of modelling in which models register their names with a company, which shows their details to clients and finds them work.

brand loyalty – loyalty given by consumers to a particular product made by a particular manufacturer. Advertising agencies and manufacturers spend a lot of time and money trying to convince customers to buy a specific product rather than alternatives produced by rival companies.

buyer – a person employed to buy merchandise for a shop or department store.

catwalk – the raised platform that models walk up and down at fashion shows to display clothes.

chain store – one of a number of retail outlets under the same ownership and management.

chisel – a tool used for working wood, consisting of a flat blade with a cutting edge attached to a handle.

chrome – a hard, grey, shiny metal.

commissioned – being employed by a company to do a specific job.

computer-aided design – design work carried out on computer using specific software programmes. These allow designers to visualize their ideas on screen before beginning work on the real thing.

designer label – a range of clothes created by a well known designer and carrying his or her name, usually on a label sewn into the garment. Such clothes are sold in exclusive shops at high prices.

editor – a person who prepares written material for publication.

freelance – self employment, working for a range of different people rather than being employed by a single company.

haute couture – high fashion, the most expensive level of the fashion industry involving individual designs for the very rich and famous.

henna – a reddish dye obtained from the powdered leaves of a plant found in Asia and North Africa.

high street fashion – affordable clothes sold to ordinary people in shops in town and city centres.

installation – setting up, construction. Used to describe a type of retail display, for example, in a shop window.

kohl – a powder derived from the chemical element antimony, and used to darken the eyelids and eyelashes.

lens – a piece of glass in a camera that controls the transmission of light to produce optical images.

mannequin – a life-size dummy model of the human body used to fit or display clothes.

paisley – a pattern of small, curving shapes with intricate detailing.

Polaroid – a photo produced by a Polariod camera. Photographs can be developed and processed inside this type of camera and take only a few seconds to produce.

portfolio – a flat case containing drawings or photographs that demonstrate recent work.

ready-to-wear – another name for designer label clothes, sold in small numbers in expensive shops.

runway – another name for a catwalk.

separates – skirts, trousers, jumpers, blouses and tops.

showroom modelling – a type of modelling in which models are permanently employed by a design company.

subtle – not immediately obvious.

three-dimensional – describes an object which has length, breadth and depth.

venue – a place where a gathering or event, such as a fashion show, is held.

Further Information

So do you still want to work in fashion?

This book aims to give you an idea of the range of different jobs in the fashion industry, and what working in it is really like. The fashion world is exciting and fast-moving and can be very glamorous. However, it's important to remember that there are far more people wanting to work in the fashion industry than there are jobs for them.

It takes talent, hard work, determination and a great deal of luck to succeed as a fashion model, make-up artist, designer, journalist or photographer. Equally, jobs as display designers and retail buyers demand good qualifications and practical talent.

Retail selling careers in fashion shops and departments are not covered in this book, but they do offer good opportunities to young people with enthusiasm and energy.

The way to find out if a job in fashion is right for you is to find out as much as you can about such work. If you are at secondary school and seriously interested in a career in fashion, ask your careers teacher if he or she can arrange some work experience for you. This means spending some time, usually a week or two, in a shop, a manufacturing operation, or a fashion house.

Books

If you want to find out about working in fashion, you will find the following helpful:

Real Life Guides: Hairdressing, written by Dee Pilgrim, published by Trotman, 2003.

Working in Fashion, published by Connexions, 2003.

Working in Retail, published by Connexions, 2001.

Working in Photography, published by Connexions, 2001.

weblinks

For websites relevant to this book, go to www.waylinks.co.uk/series/soyouwant/fashion

Useful addresses

United Kingdom

Fashion Make-up and Hair Styling

Hairdressing and Beauty
Industry Authority
Fraser House
Nether Hall Road
Doncaster
DN1 2PH
Tel: 01302 380000

Modelling

Association of Model
Agents
122 Brompton Road
London
SW3 1JD
Tel: 020 7564 6466

Fashion Design

London College of Fashion
20 John Prince's Street
London
W1G 0BJ
Tel: 020 7514 7400

Edinburgh College of Art
Lauriston Place
Edinburgh
EH3 9DF
Tel: 01331 221 6000

Retail Buying

Chartered Institute of
Purchasing and Supply
Easton House
Easton on the Hill
Stamford
PE9 3NZ
Tel: 01780 756777

Skillsmart Retail Ltd
The Retail Sector Skills
Council
21 Dartmouth Street
London
SW1H 9BP
Tel: 020 7854 8900

Fashion Photography

The Association of
Photographers
81 Leonard Street
London
EC2A 4QS
Tel: 020 7739 6669

British Institute of
Professional Photography
Fox Talbot House
2 Amwell End
Ware
Hertfordshire
SG12 9HN
Tel: 01920 464011

Fashion Journalism

National Council for the
Training of Journalists
Latton Bush Centre
Southern Way
Harlow
Essex
CM18 7BL
Tel: 01279 430009

Australia

National Training
Information Service
Australian National
Training Authority
Level 17
200 Mary Street
Brisbane
QLD 4001
GPO Box 3120
Tel (07) 3246 2300

National Training
Information Service
5/321 Exhibition Street
Melbourne VIC 3000
GPO Box 5347BB
Melbourne VIC 3001
Tel (03) 9630 9800

New Zealand

kiwicareers.govt.nz
Tel: 0800 222733

Index